THE

DON'T
LAUGH

CHALLENGE

Joke Book

Easter Edition

2020

An Interactive Easter-Themed Joke Book Contest for Boys, Girls, and Kids Ages 7-12

4

Don't Laugh Challenge
BONUS PLAY

Join our Joke Club and get the Bonus Play PDF!

Simply send us an email to:

 bacchuspublish@gmail.com

and you will get the following:

• 10 BONUS hilarious jokes!

• An entry in our Monthly Giveaway of a
$25 Amazon Gift card!

We draw a new winner each month and will contact you via email!

Good luck!

Welcome to
The Don't Laugh Challenge™

• How do you play?

The Don't Laugh Challenge is made up of 10 rounds with 2 games in each round. It is a 2-3 player game with the players being 'Jester #1','Jester #2', and a 'King' or 'Queen'. In each game you have an opportunity to score points by making the other players laugh.

After completing each round, tally up the points to determine the Round Champion! Add all 10 rounds together to see who is the Ultimate Don't Laugh Challenge Master! If you end up in a tie, use our final Tie Breaker Round for a Winner Takes All!

• Who can play the game?

Get the whole family involved! Grab a family member or a friend and take turns going back and forth. We've also added Bonus Points in game 2, so grab a 3rd person, a.k.a 'King' or 'Queen', and earn an extra point by making them guess your scene!

The Don't Laugh Challenge™ Activity Rules

- ## Game 1 - Jokes (1 point each)

  Jester #1 will hold the book and read each joke to Jester #2. If the joke makes Jester #2 laugh, Jester #1 can record a point for the joke. Each joke is worth 1 point. At the end of the jokes, tally up your total Joke Points scored for Jester #1 and continue to Game 2!

- ## Game 2 - Silly Scenarios (2 points each + bonus point)

  Without telling the other Jester what the scenarios say, read each scenario to yourself and then get creative by acting it out! You can use sound effects, but be sure not to say any words! If you make the other Jester laugh, record your points and continue to the next scenario.

  BONUS POINT: Get your parents or a third player, a.k.a King or Queen, involved and have them guess what in the world you are doing! Get the King or Queen to guess the scene correctly and you score a BONUS POINT!

The Don't Laugh Challenge™
Activity Rules

Once Jester #1 completes both games it is Jester #2's turn. The directions at the bottom of the book will tell you who goes next. Once you have both completed all the games in the round, add your total points from each game to the Round Score Page and record the Round winner!

- ## How do you get started?

  Flip a coin. If guessed correctly, then that Jester begins!

  Tip: Make any of the activities extra funny by using facial expressions, funny voices or silly movements!

ROUND

Jokes

How do rabbits like their gold?

With 24 carrots!

/1

What do you call a royal chicken?

'King HEN-ry.'

/1

Why did the Easter Bunny go jogging?

He was getting his EGG-ercise!

/1

Why was the dog so happy to be on a horse-drawn carriage?

/1

They were on a WAG-on!

JOKES TOTAL: _____ /4

JESTER 1 CONTINUE TO THE NEXT PAGE

Silly Scenarios

(Act it out!)

You're the Easter Bunny and it's time to hide all your eggs! Twitch your whiskers and chomp your front teeth while hopping around and hiding eggs!

/2

You are a karate master! After bowing to the crowd, you start to kick, chop, and spin! Shout while you move and make intense faces to show you mean business!

/2

SILLY SCENARIOS TOTAL: _____ /4

NOW, PASS THE BOOK TO JESTER 2 ➔

Jokes

Why did the egg need a long vacation?

He was CRACKING under pressure!

/1

What do you call a cartoon about fruit?

Banana-mation!

/1

What's a pitcher's favorite candy bar?

Mounds!

/1

What did the chicken go to college for?

EGG-counting.

/1

JOKES TOTAL: _____ /4

JESTER 2 CONTINUE TO THE NEXT PAGE ➞

14

Silly Scenarios

(Act it out!)

Pretend you're competing in an Easter candy contest and try to eat as much candy in 30 seconds as you can! Once you're done, pretend to have a sugar rush and run around the room!

_____ /2

You have an unusual allergy, every time you look at your phone you fall asleep! Now try to check your text messages and message someone back, but your eyes will barely stay open!

_____ /2

SILLY SCENARIOS TOTAL: _____ /4

TIME TO SCORE YOUR POINTS!

JESTER 1

 /8

ROUND TOTAL

JESTER 2

/8

ROUND TOTAL

ROUND
CHAMPION

ROUND

Jokes

Why didn't the eggs go out and party?

They were totally BEAT.

_____ /1

How did the chickens stop fighting?

They learned how to COOP-erate!

_____ /1

What do you call a church made up of falcons?

'Birds of Pray.'

_____ /1

How does the Easter Bunny get rid of termites?

He EGGS-terminates them!

_____ /1

JOKES TOTAL: _____ /4

JESTER 1 CONTINUE TO THE NEXT PAGE

Silly Scenarios

(Act it out!)

Your feet hurt! Crawl or roll around the room on your knees, elbows, and stomach! If you stand up on your feet, cry out in pain (silently, but dramatically)!

/2

Come up with your own spy music to hum while you roll, jump, and sneak around the room. Try and take an object in the room and move it somewhere else, as sneakily as possible!

/2

SILLY SCENARIOS TOTAL: _____ /4

Jokes

What do board games eat for breakfast?

Scrabbled eggs!

/1

Why was the flower a natural born leader?

She always ROSE to the occasion.

/1

What kind of soda does Pocahontas drink?

Poca-Cola!

/1

Why did the mother hen have to separate her chicks?

They kept EGG-ing each other on!

/1

JOKES TOTAL: _____ /4

JESTER 2 CONTINUE TO THE NEXT PAGE ➤

20

Silly Scenarios

(Act it out!)

There is one delicious gumdrop left on the gumdrop tree, but it's just out of reach! Try to jump, poke, throw or shake anything to knock it down!

/2

Imagine you're a fly stuck in a spider's web, and the more you try to escape the stickier it becomes! UH-OH... here comes the spider! Give your best scared face as you frantically try to get away!

/2

SILLY SCENARIOS TOTAL: _____ /4

TIME TO SCORE YOUR POINTS!

JESTER 1

/8

ROUND TOTAL

JESTER 2

/8

ROUND TOTAL

ROUND
CHAMPION

ROUND

3

Jokes

Why do trained dogs make excellent doctors?

They're good at HEEL-ing.

_____ /1

Why does hopscotch often get ignored?

It's easy to skip over!

_____ /1

What's the Easter Bunny's second favorite vegetable after carrots?

Eggplants!

_____ /1

Why did the pig stop jogging?

He hurt his HAM-string!

_____ /1

JOKES TOTAL: _____ /4

JESTER 1 CONTINUE TO THE NEXT PAGE ➡

Silly Scenarios

(Act it out!)

You're a pet rabbit that has a bad case of the fleas! You're super itchy and trying to scratch that itch, while running away from your frantic owner who keeps chasing you!

/2

Let's see your best invisible piano recital! Use your fingers to play the keyboard while using your body and head to show you are lost in the music! Give a performance worthy of a standing ovation!

/2

SILLY SCENARIOS TOTAL: _____ /4

NOW, PASS THE BOOK TO JESTER 2 ➔

Jokes

What's the most annoying kind of egg?

A practical yolker!

/1

Why did the lizard push the monkey?

He's cold-blooded.

/1

What do you get when you combine a chicken and a centipede together?

A whole lot of drumsticks!

/1

What did the tree say after the party?

"I'm gonna STICK around for a few more minutes!"

/1

JOKES TOTAL: _____ /4

JESTER 2 CONTINUE TO THE NEXT PAGE →

26

Silly Scenarios

(Act it out!)

It's a windy day and you're holding onto your umbrella for dear life, when suddenly a strong gust of wind blows you around and around! Try to stop getting pushed by the wind, but don't let your umbrella go!

/2

You are making a pot of tea. You gently pour some tea into a cup and lift it to your mouth to take a sip - Pinky out! When you do take a sip, you immediately realize it is WAY too hot and you spit it out in the most dramatic way!

/2

SILLY SCENARIOS TOTAL: /4

TIME TO SCORE YOUR POINTS!

JESTER 1

$/8$

ROUND TOTAL

JESTER 2

$/8$

ROUND TOTAL

ROUND
CHAMPION

ROUND

Jokes

Why was the apple in such great shape?

It was always working on its **CORE!**

_____ /1

What is Starbuck's favorite musical artist?

Ariana **GRANDE.**

_____ /1

Why was the egg not good at sports?

Because it always cracked under pressure!

_____ /1

Which candy loves the playground?

_____ /1

RECESS Pieces!

JOKES TOTAL: _____ /4

JESTER 1 CONTINUE TO THE NEXT PAGE

Silly Scenarios

(Act it out!)

You're a determined rabbit that is in a rush to eat all the carrots from your garden.
Hop around, grab one carrot at a time, and eat them with as many small nibbles as it takes!

/2

You are a runway model going down the catwalk, but it's your first time! Meow every time you take a step, then strike a glamorous pose and give a loud HISS to show some attitude!

/2

SILLY SCENARIOS TOTAL: _____ /4

NOW, PASS THE BOOK TO JESTER 2 ➜

Jokes

Where do cows go when they get sick?

The FARM-acy!

/1

What food is always grumpy?

SOUR cream.

/1

How do you know trees are fans of apples?

They are always ROOTING for them!

/1

What kind of eggs does a dog get on Easter?

Pooched eggs!

/1

JOKES TOTAL: _____ /4

JESTER 2 CONTINUE TO THE NEXT PAGE ➞

Silly Scenarios

(Act it out!)

While hiding Easter eggs outside, you notice a carrot sticking out of the ground. When you try to pull it, it keeps getting longer and longer... IT'S NEVER ENDING! Keep pulling until you get the whole carrot out, then plop down to the ground from exhaustion!

_____ /2

You're a cowboy riding on your horse and you accidentally lasso yourself! Whoops! Try your best to get out of the tight grip!

_____ /2

SILLY SCENARIOS TOTAL: _____ /4

TIME TO SCORE YOUR POINTS!

JESTER 1

/8

ROUND TOTAL

JESTER 2

/8

ROUND TOTAL

ROUND
CHAMPION

ROUND

Jokes

Why did the farmer hire a helper?

He didn't have enough THYME! _____ /1

What kind of day is it when rabbits misbehave?

A bad HARE day! _____ /1

Why wouldn't you want to sit next to a chicken at school?

They constantly PEEP at your homework! _____ /1

What do you call two dogs that are working together for the science fair?

LAB partners!

JOKES TOTAL: _____ /4

JESTER 1 CONTINUE TO THE NEXT PAGE

Silly Scenarios

(Act it out!)

You are riding a crazy roller coaster for the 10th time in a row! Once you stop, you're so dizzy that you trip, stumble and walk in circles trying to find the exit!

_____ /2

HANG TEN! You're the first bunny to ever attempt surfing a giant wave... while also doing the floss dance!!!

_____ /2

SILLY SCENARIOS TOTAL: _____ /4

NOW, PASS THE BOOK TO JESTER 2 ➡

Jokes

What do you call a Star Wars chef?

'Baking Yoda.'

/1

What did the egg say after finishing a simple test?

"Over! Easy."

/1

What does Nutella do to get on a sandwich?

He gets BREAD-y!

/1

Why did the rabbit get in trouble?

He was playing with matchstick carrots!

/1

JOKES TOTAL: _____ /4

JESTER 2 CONTINUE TO THE NEXT PAGE

Silly Scenarios

(Act it out!)

Hop across the floor like a bunny with a case of the hiccups, but they're so bad that you nearly flip over or fall every time you hiccup!

/2

You have 30 seconds to find the frog prince, but you keep kissing the wrong one and their tongues keep getting stuck to your face! EW!

/2

SILLY SCENARIOS TOTAL: _____ /4

TIME TO SCORE YOUR POINTS! ➜

39

JESTER 1

 /8

ROUND TOTAL

JESTER 2

/8

ROUND TOTAL

ROUND
CHAMPION

ROUND

Jokes

What kind of vegetable loves to take selfies?

Snap peas!

/1

Why is the farmer always talking to the cornfield?

Because it's all EARS!

/1

How do chickens get off the road?

They take an EGGS-it!

/1

Why did the pony borrow money?

He was a bit short.

/1

JOKES TOTAL: _____ /4

JESTER 1 CONTINUE TO THE NEXT PAGE

42

Silly Scenarios

(Act it out!)

You're a tightrope walker walking against a strong wind. Do your best to stay balanced, but show how hard it is with crazy facial expressions!

/2

You just stepped out of your car into a HUGE rainstorm! Now try to fight the wind and reach the door to your home, without losing your umbrella!

/2

SILLY SCENARIOS TOTAL: _____ /4

NOW, PASS THE BOOK TO JESTER 2 ➡

43

Jokes

What kind of bird is best at dodgeball?

Duck!

/1

Why did the chickens lose the basketball game?

Too many fowls!

/1

What is the Easter Bunny's favorite Olympic sport?

Hopscotch.

/1

What video game console is used for praying?

A PRAY-station.

/1

JOKES TOTAL: _____ /4

JESTER 2 CONTINUE TO THE NEXT PAGE ➡️

Silly Scenarios

(Act it out!)

Fashion show time, but the floor is covered in sticky, melted marshmallows! Show how you strut your stuff while doing your best to make it down the sticky runway and back without falling!

/2

You're a very excited puppy, whose owner has taken you to the park! Show your friend your newly learned tricks! (Shake, roll over, jump, etc.)

/2

SILLY SCENARIOS TOTAL: _____ /4

TIME TO SCORE YOUR POINTS!

JESTER 1

/8

ROUND TOTAL

JESTER 2

/8

ROUND TOTAL

ROUND
CHAMPION

ROUND

7

Jokes

Why shouldn't you take a cat seriously?

They're always KITTEN around!

/1

What do you call it when a cow remembers something new?

'Déjà Moo.'

/1

Why did the wad of bubblegum extend his vacation?

/1

He wanted to STICK around longer!

Why are flowers so popular?

/1

They have the best BUDS.

JOKES TOTAL: _____ /4

JESTER 1 CONTINUE TO THE NEXT PAGE ➡

Silly Scenarios

(Act it out!)

You drop everything you pick up! Today, you're helping someone move all of their glass cups, bowls and plates. Keep trying to pick it up and move it in the box, but drop each item until finally you get frustrated and run away dramatically!

/2

Uh-oh! Your favorite shirt just came out of the dryer and it shrunk to doll size! You are still determined to put it on, but don't forget to show what a struggle it is!

/2

SILLY SCENARIOS TOTAL: _____ /4

NOW, PASS THE BOOK TO JESTER 2 ➡

Jokes

What board game do rabbits love?

HOP-eration!

_____ /1

Why was the baby cow so hyper?

It had too much CALF-eine.

_____ /1

What do you call a dog that can catch a football?

A Golden Receiver.

_____ /1

Why did the Easter Bunny join the library?

Because he loves to BURROW things!

_____ /1

JOKES TOTAL: _____ /4

50

JESTER 2 CONTINUE TO THE NEXT PAGE

Silly Scenarios

(Act it out!)

Pretend you're the Easter Bunny and are trying to hide eggs around the room without your friend noticing. Every time they look at you, freeze and hop away like nothing happened! Keep trying until you've successfully hidden 3 eggs!

_____ /2

You're all dressed up and ready to go! Oops! You've tied your shoelaces together by mistake. Hop like a bunny to the nearest seat, so you don't trip!

_____ /2

SILLY SCENARIOS TOTAL: _____ /4

TIME TO SCORE YOUR POINTS!

JESTER 1

/8

_____

ROUND TOTAL

JESTER 2

/8

_____

ROUND TOTAL

_____

ROUND
CHAMPION

ROUND

Jokes

Why was the fried chicken afraid to cross the street?

There was a spork in the road!

/1

Why was the horse late?

It kept STALL-ing!

/1

Where do sheep go shopping?

BAAH-ttery Barn.

/1

What is the Easter Bunny's favorite restaurant?

IHOP.

/1

JOKES TOTAL: _____ /4

JESTER 1 CONTINUE TO THE NEXT PAGE ➡

54

Silly Scenarios

(Act it out!)

You're in a strong man competition and all you have to do now is the power lift. Just as you bend down to lift, a loud toot escapes! Drop the weight from embarrassment and tip-toe away!

/2

Oops! You're the Easter Bunny, but you forgot where you hid the eggs and Easter is coming! Dig frantically and search all over, but you just can't remember where you put them!

/2

SILLY SCENARIOS TOTAL: _____ /4

NOW, PASS THE BOOK TO JESTER 2 ➡

Jokes

Who do farm animals talk to when they have trouble with a bully?

The school COW-nselor.

/1

How often do hens lay eggs?

EGGS-actly as often as they'd like!

/1

What is a dog's favorite perfume scent?

Lavend-FUR!

/1

Who is a llama's favorite musical artist?

/1

LLAMA Del Rey.

JOKES TOTAL: _____ /4

JESTER 2 CONTINUE TO THE NEXT PAGE

Silly Scenarios

(Act it out!)

As you are combing your hair and getting ready for Easter with the family, you notice there's slime stuck in your hair! You try to get it out, but it keeps sticking to your fingers! Act disgusted and try really hard to get your hand unstuck!

_/2

While hopping on one foot, use your imaginary water hose to put out a giant wildfire!

_/2

SILLY SCENARIOS TOTAL:_____ /4

TIME TO SCORE YOUR POINTS!

JESTER 1

/8

ROUND TOTAL

JESTER 2

/8

ROUND TOTAL

ROUND CHAMPION

ROUND

Jokes

What did the main character in the Easter play say to the playwright?

"Get your ACT together!"

/1

How do dogs use the phone?

They call the PAW-perator.

/1

Why couldn't the bug drive?

He didn't have a LICE-nse!

/1

What was the bird's favorite game?

Anything that TOUCAN play together!

/1

JOKES TOTAL: _____ /4

JESTER 1 CONTINUE TO THE NEXT PAGE

Silly Scenarios

(Act it out!)

You're stuck in an Easter video game as a character of your choice! Loudly announce every action before you do it and make sure to be super animated!

/2

Be a lazy cat. Lay down, stretch, make purring or meowing noises, and playfully paw at other players!

/2

SILLY SCENARIOS TOTAL: _____ /4

NOW, PASS THE BOOK TO JESTER 2 ➡

Jokes

Which talk show host is a favorite amongst birds?

Jimmy FALCON!

/1

Why did the Easter Bunny make an appointment at the salon?

He needed a HARE cut!

/1

What sets in when a wild pig has nothing to do?

BOAR-dom.

/1

How do birds connect to the internet?

They use wi-FLY!

/1

JOKES TOTAL: _____ /4

JESTER 2 CONTINUE TO THE NEXT PAGE ➜

Silly Scenarios

(Act it out!)

JESTER 2

You are a loud chicken giving yourself a bath. Cluck your favorite song while you do it! (Tip: Make chicken-like head movements and use your arms for wings!)

_____ /2

Pretend you're the Easter Bunny and you're about to play your favorite game... Hopscotch! Jump awkwardly to each box while keeping your hands at your chest, like a bunny, then finish it off with the floss!

_____ /2

SILLY SCENARIOS TOTAL: _____ /4

TIME TO SCORE YOUR POINTS!

JESTER 1

/8

ROUND TOTAL

JESTER 2

/8

ROUND TOTAL

ROUND
CHAMPION

ROUND

10

Jokes

What kind of dress does a mattress look best in?

A SPRING dress!

/1

Why was the rabbit so apathetic?

He didn't CARROT all!

/1

What do you call baby lions on top of a mother lion?

A backpack!

/1

Why did no one drink the cow's milk?

It was PASTURE expiration date!

/1

JOKES TOTAL: _____ /4

JESTER 1 CONTINUE TO THE NEXT PAGE

Silly Scenarios

(Act it out!)

You are the Easter Bunny and have a super itchy back! Without using your hands, try and scratch it the best you can!

_____ /2

Become a strip of bacon being made for breakfast! Pretend to throw yourself in the pan, and sizzle until you're all done and crispy!

_____ /2

SILLY SCENARIOS TOTAL: _____ /4

NOW, PASS THE BOOK TO JESTER 2 ➡

Jokes

Why did the egg become a detective?

It was good at CRACKING the code.

/1

Why is theater so much fun?

The play!

/1

Knock knock!
Who's there?
Common.
Common, who?
Common, open the door!

/1

Did you know that frogs secretly wish they were bunnies?

That's why they hop around saying, "Rabbit, rabbit!"

/1

JOKES TOTAL: _____ /4

JESTER 2 CONTINUE TO THE NEXT PAGE ➡

Silly Scenarios

(Act it out!)

Your shoes love to dance, but you don't. What would it look like if your feet were dancing around, but your body and face showed you didn't want to? Get to dancing and show the crowd!

_____/2

Act like a mimicking parrot that repeats what it hears. Make sure to copy anything that anyone says in the room with a bird voice and move your body around like one, too!

_____/2

SILLY SCENARIOS TOTAL: _____/4

TIME TO SCORE YOUR POINTS!

JESTER 1

/8

_____
ROUND TOTAL

JESTER 2

/8

_____
ROUND TOTAL

_____

ROUND
CHAMPION

ADD UP ALL YOUR POINTS FROM EACH ROUND.
THE PLAYER WITH THE MOST POINTS IS CROWNED
THE ULTIMATE DON'T LAUGH CHALLENGE MASTER!

IN THE EVENT OF A TIE, CONTINUE TO THE
ROUND 11 FOR THE TIE-BREAKER ROUND!

JESTER 1

_____
GRAND TOTAL

JESTER 2

_____
GRAND TOTAL

_____

THE ULTIMATE
DON'T LAUGH CHALLENGE MASTER

ROUND

11

Tie-Breaker
(Winner Takes All!)

Jokes

Will you be joining the school's gardening club?

Yes, I PLANT to!

/1

Who do fish see when they are hurt?

The Nurse Shark.

/1

What kind of car does a hen like to lay her eggs in?

HATCH-back.

/1

What do you say to a jockey who's in a rush?

"Hold your horses!"

/1

JOKES TOTAL: _____ /4

JESTER 1 CONTINUE TO THE NEXT PAGE ➡

Silly Scenarios

(Act it out!)

You're in the middle of your Easter Championship hockey game, when suddenly your hockey stick turns into a wet noodle! Try to keep playing anyway!

/2

Just as you're about to take a sip of your morning orange juice, a miniature rabbit leaps out of it! That was weird... you try to take another sip, but each time **ANOTHER** rabbit jumps out! Drop your cup and act super confused!

/2

SILLY SCENARIOS TOTAL: _____ /4

NOW, PASS THE BOOK TO JESTER 2 ➜

Jokes

What kind of Easter egg travels down the Amazon?

An EGGS-plorer!

/1

What body style of car do chickens love?

Coops.

/1

Why did the Easter Bunny have to leave school?

He was EGG-spelled!

/1

What's a chicken's favorite vegetable?

BAWK-Choy!

/1

JOKES TOTAL: _____ /4

JESTER 2 CONTINUE TO THE NEXT PAGE ➡

Silly Scenarios

(Act it out!)

Pretend you're the Easter Bunny, but while hopping around you quickly realize you are sinking in quicksand! UH-OH! Try to pull yourself out of the sand pit as you slowly get dragged in deeper and deeper!

___ /2

You try a new lotion that smells and tastes amazing! It smells so good, that every time you apply more, you try to lick it off your own skin! Keep applying more!

___ /2

SILLY SCENARIOS TOTAL: ___ /4

TIME TO SCORE YOUR POINTS! ➡

ADD UP ALL YOUR POiNTS FROM THE PREViOUS ROUND. THE JESTER WiTH THE MOST POiNTS iS CROWNED THE ULTIMATE DON'T LAUGH CHALLENGE MASTER!

JESTER 1

/8

GRAND TOTAL

JESTER 2

/8

GRAND TOTAL

THE ULTIMATE DON'T LAUGH CHALLENGE MASTER

Check out our

Visit us at
www.DontLaughChallenge.com
to check out our newest books!

other joke books!

If you have enjoyed our book, we would love for you to review us on Amazon!

Made in the USA
Monee, IL
18 March 2020

23233008R00046